NIGHT-
SEA

✺

RACHEL
MORITZ

NIGHT-
SEA

✼

RACHEL
MORITZ

NEW MICHIGAN PRESS
TUCSON, ARIZONA

NEW MICHIGAN PRESS
DEPT OF ENGLISH, P. O. BOX 210067
UNIVERSITY OF ARIZONA
TUCSON, AZ 85721-0067

<http://newmichiganpress.com/nmp>

Orders and queries to nmp@thediagram.com.

Copyright © 2008 by Rachel Moritz.
All rights reserved.

ISBN 978-1-934832-16-5. FIRST PRINTING.

Printed in the United States of America.

Design by Ander Monson.

Cover photo: [Cast of Abraham Lincoln's hands lying on a plain backdrop], DN-0005719, *Chicago Daily News* negatives collection, Chicago Historical Society. Used by permission.

CONTENTS

I   Abduction, 5
    And Each Man Is, 8
    Elixir (to Guide You), 10
    Initiation, 12
    Wonder Journey (Air-Wind), 14
    With His Son, 16
    Whale Belly (a Series of Trials), 17

II Apotheosis, 21
    Paternity, 23
    Magic Flight, 24
    Threshold Struggle, 26
    Defeat, 28
    Past the World of the Senses, 29
    Melancholia, 30
    Silences of the Personal, 31
    Maternity, 32
    Letters Home, 33

III Premonitions, 37
    At the Hospital, 39
    High Spirits, 41
    Scaffolding, 42
    My Childhood Home I See Again, 43
    Return, 44
    Emanations-Dissolutions, 45

    Notes & Acknowledgments, 49

❋

"And so it happens that if anyone—in any society—undertakes for himself the perilous journey into the darkness by descending, either intentionally or unintentionally, into the crooked landscape of symbolical figures … this is the process of dissolving, transcending or transmuting the infantile images of our personal past."

—Joseph Campbell

"Herewith is a little sketch, as you requested. There is not much of it, for the reason, I suppose, that there is not much of me."

—Abraham Lincoln, 1859

I

*

ABDUCTION

1

Wolves howled at night.
How people's faces change.
One room, one window and one door.
The short and simple annals of the poor.
Who die of milk fever.
A naiveté in his manner and voice produced a strange
    effect on his audience.
No other marks or brands recollected.
He is tired and worn out.
Such a homely face.
This one discovers the sadness of his soul.
This one tells of his determined spirit.
Outside—a little blurred figure in rain.
The train moves on.
The train moves toward the future.

2

Then I dreamed in elm
acres and valleys, land drought-

swollen, in cellars minted
by repetitive descent.

As we can't love our own
image, we find one
opposite to whitewash.

Mine was sentencing
indefinite surrender,
the kind you always resist.

Couldn't see my witness, but knew
he stood at my back as I slept,

his touch the four soft corners
of the palm, expelling my shattered mind
and moving onward.

Bowels of his inside: where cabin logs
were fenced and born.

Full round of fallow
earth before the world comes
to retrieve him.

O yes, he says, in your bark ferry, desirous

of my known craft, you who are
listening—

. . .

Tree: rebirth

Mirror: field of the reflected

AND EACH MAN IS

I almost died, three years old
at the range in Boston, running out in shotguns' path.

But that was the 1970s,
and things were looser then.

Your rifles propped in golden oil
both frightening and good.

You liked to clean them
with a cotton rag, because you were a man born
in the mid-twentieth century.

Later, your migraines and the living room
was suffering. Rain fell
against the walls of our house.

Maybe you loved the target's glowing eye,
down below in the moldy basement.

Maybe your carried your holster through the house,
after a dinner of meatloaf.

You clipped the long dead gray men from a Xerox,
taped their eyes above your desk.

How much nostalgia lives
inside rusty bullets, amputation kits.

This idea of the 'great moment' and the 'hero'—

ELIXIR
(TO GUIDE YOU)

1

The first emanation is the head itself, in profile.

And from this process, 'nine splendid lights.'

Black hair, high on a porcelain brow.

Eyes of the beaten dog,

roads paved past jaw.

So many forms and none can you pin. How he changes.

How war ages.

Nine revealing portraits, this one in reflective pose.

This one shows the man who knows a dark side of life.

Our vessel, withered travail.

. . .

"I saw my own body move across the waters"
"There was a dark and indefinite shore"
"I never felt so happy as when going there"

2

His profile, incubus mouth. Cloud
and mist of the belly. What were his veins
now our rivers. What was fluid within
his eyes now our tears. What was membrane
of the skull now our fragmented plethora.

Our earth, broken. Our word-
smith, our elected host.

We climb the vessel with each great face
of the world and find our own—

'half alligator, half horse'

INITIATION

Did you know the first woman hung
in America was the owner

of that lodging-house where Booth
and the others plotted?

Cloth billowing, rope
around her ankles.

And Lincoln with his terminal answer, his barge
floating hours before death.

All those men in history
like vegetables drained of fluid.

The little shoes they wear with neither
left nor right sides.

Thus begins my love for the past which carries
long epitaph—

Lewis, the half-wit, only twenty years
of age and wrestling with Secretary Seward's son.

Back then men wore
names like 'half-wit' and 'hero'—

She asserted to the end
her innocence, high collar
black patterned brow.

These four hanged, these four imprisoned.

And the past was a tunnel you did not visit.
A zero at the tunnel's hinge.

WONDER JOURNEY
(AIR-WIND)

"Above the broad, unmoving depths, beneath the nine spheres and the seven floors of heaven, at the central point, where the moon does not wane."

. . .

Each winter day is dream-
like in duration.

More abstractly still, each
is a brooding self, absolute

to the act of creation.

Out of two mirrored eyebrows
at dawn, one silver

the other red
as his wife's halo.

Either way what you desire
is darkness, tossed

between waking,
dream and deeper sentiment.

All share one landscape
who survives.

Wind, carrion,
crows staring the ridge

whose overhang is cloud
never fully upon us.

In snow walking
paths beneath the highway,

great vehicles of oil rush
your animal name.

What is form but a moment
coalescing?

. . .

Oaring your body across

that brief monologue.

WITH HIS SON

Look at the father's care
holding a book on his lap
and the son with oiled cowlick and watch
slipped from breastpocket.

These two are a portrait of—?

The book is my first held
child, its luminous ocean and hillside,
its library of slender paperbacks.

Each boy inside the book
wanders by sea, escorting gulls
and ripe fruit he chews inside,
carried up to the heavens.

I love James. He's a boy,
unlike me.

Now he's 55, my Lincoln, on February 9th.
He is twenty-two years older than me.
Now his youngest named Tad
(dropsy of the chest)
at the book with father
and Matthew Brady.

**WHALE BELLY
(A SERIES OF TRIALS)**

The room behind your back turns
on its axis, not before it.

You lie infantile,
averting your navel from the door.

And where are you going,
my only winter guide?

"To hell, I suppose," he said of his marriage. Her headaches
came—and violently came—

This self cannot be cut nor
withered, only rode out.

So you write, while waiting,
a letter on gilded canvas.

Your pen leaks, like the mind.

So you find your answer in rain
laterally washing his address.

Where cameras obscure
the tops of their heads

is movement,
beginning even then.

II

✺

APOTHEOSIS

Deftly an arrow 'shot'
and man's biography, fallen
at tree line.

A few feet away keels
the mythic shelter.

Each home remedial,
gnawed out of forest

while the day licks
sallow the fields.

Milk fever of 'begot'
and 'begotten.'

A woman was needed in the house—

. . .

He walked to an oak at the edge of Indian wood and from the trunk arose a maiden, eager to cure his loss. Why have you come? You (he) ask the divine. Onto the melancholy sheet of your face, her gaze an emblem of the infinite. How the hewn doorway proceeds with slant, the gate at the creek grows feeble.

Have you earned your dollar by ferrying his fortune from one dimension to the next? Her half-digested leaf in your mouth, her vessels the water's rise, her hair the corn strands of mid-country dusk. Her neighboring voice fells the axe in your heart, her yawning the lightening of keys to this ongoing.

. . .

3 AM: a barge

soars the lake, gestating

oar-belly of city

Granite before trees who are not here

for miles

PATERNITY

A depression behind the eye
procured more

who knew what that word meant.

Our particular kind of puncheon
floor and well-

greased prairie window,

a thousand men
buckling their belts

clamor escape
or amorous inclinations.

Someone rode a pony in the garden, stood

as sage behind
his father's death-bed.

Mine wiled away the night with headache
—dark as forest, dark as dragon—

ghetto before brick or trowel
with my name on it.

MAGIC FLIGHT

A camera records the great events of his life.
So is photojournalism born.

Blacktopped hats and snow
drizzling the capital.

Our flag now
wears thirty-four stars.

In the morning we board a ferry that sings
the bay into Lantau—

sun muscling
behind the mountains

and what's behind us in water
is your life in names, did you call me

here to be, did I call myself?

Drinking from sweet boxes
of Vita Soy,

we are little owned frames
who squat deliberate

in the body's steam,
fling the boxes of urine into waves.

Meanwhile Lincoln on his way
to the Capital,

the flag at Antietam stays
a single wooden post

and inside he sits at a table
wishing his generals luck.

I am a square who has drunk herself
clean on the deck holding

soy milk in a paper box.

Memory, as we empty,
and the ocean where waves go

—shaking hands and wishing—

this singular hello.

THRESHOLD STRUGGLE

That was only soil
they tended,

not the soul
unsought.

First air turns to fire
and then a third

element spills
behind life, shaping the lake

uncovered as snow is now
skeletal—shoreline face—

newly loosened
by the act of dream.

Don't go too far, your doorway motions,
bathed in light from nowhere,

if only for revelation, what the mind
already knows—

that time is a triangle we all coexist
in, if we see the sentence

in periphery, who would sail forward
and who would sail back home?

Lake waves, frenetic, pulse beyond us into that last

element, that which purely configures
the earth.

DEFEAT

Each posture upright while it walked,

medals pinning the wool

stank of horse flesh.

As wheels turned, the back of a lens.

All the faces simply who were

gray where colors bled.

I was tired waiting for knowledge,

blue cloaks my frost besieged.

I had hands and fingers,

I held to madness.

Bugle notes the body is all of it,

but we are bound by distance.

PAST THE WORLD OF THE SENSES

Light snow on the capital
steps = quotidian

information, the kind we love
to exchange.

Cameras, also, recording
his address.

Our flag wears thirty-two stars.

Then visit 'The War is Over'
where soldiers loll

beneath the scaffold's human
display.

For the woman, until the end—

a ladder leans, her footing
falters.

Ghost by the wall who is
my own throat.

People are already—always—
turning away.

Waiting for them to find you
will not make you matter.

MELANCHOLIA

I guess I came bearing
some kind of self

modeled after the family sentence—leaves
sewn together with twine,

walnut juice staining trousers.

And that brooding we embraced
now is only my nuisance.

Our cabins roam unhinged
the countryside of swallows.

I help felling trees
for my excavated century,

but I am no son to that wild region.

SILENCES OF THE PERSONAL

This vehicle, child

who arrives in December and coughs
his recidivate genes into clay.

"The problem is how to keep the symbol translucent, so
that it may not block out the very light
it is supposed to convey."

What light is this burden, after each blow
it takes from him

a mist on the mind, that which we now
call by clinical name.

Maybe the eyes of his child will assist you. After all, these
windows of the soul

make definite the lentine, the lost.

A myth grows around him, but can find
no prescient forms.

MATERNITY

Scab grass, the side of shelter

through which her loneliness
grows obsolete,

and while the glove folds
the skirt slumbers

this unstable firmament.

She hustles door, floor and window
where cabin lacks,

as is the heave of her back
no longer anything

with no roads to speak of
and no one else to speak of.

She is more feral than begetting
of embrace this one

gone sanity's bone-
dark way.

LETTERS HOME

"This town is a very beautiful place. Me and father have

a nice little room to ourselves. We have two pitchers on

a washstand. The smallest one for me the largest one for

father. We have two little towels on a top of both pitchers.

The smallest one for me, the largest one for father. Me and

father have gone to two theaters the other night."

. . .

And there sat the man, with a burden on the brain
at which the world marvels

bent now with load both at heart and brain—staggering
under a blow

III

*

PREMONITIONS

I've never felt so happy in my life, he says
climbing into the carriage.

And she, myth inclines us
to believe, is nervous —

he's said the same thing the night
before Willie's death.

I suppose it's the looseness of then, bulletin
goes by word-of-mouth and men who have taken two

by ferry to Alexandria sense something
clandestine.

No, I'm not trying to make the story grand.
It's not, mostly cruel and unkind.

Or just horrific with disease,
now muffled, un-American.

Not to be held up. Not that any
time is ultimately good or evil.

Simply that the language is better, or carries
more emotion inside.

Tragedy, escape—

'Thus ever be the fate of tyrants!'

AT THE HOSPITAL

The door of the burning barn.

And that pale star from Georgia, Alexander Stephens,

barely one hundred pounds but what a force
of politic.

This is my diary of the last day.

On the night of April 14th in a room
at 453 Tenth Street.

His pulse is weak. There's nothing more we can do.

And God, his inscrutable Providence,
the future we must give to him,

and so I think of you.

Mourning doves are sleeping
under the eaves, this room

has no imagination
but for mine.

You've turned thirty-six.
And don't we all have this?

The doll-like body of yours
more human than parental.

In the bay below, ferries churn
commuters to Aberdeen.

His labored breath in moments
of silence.

The second is this, some immemorial
change though we never know

in the moment.

Give a lame man a chance, he shouts
from within.

That burning up and then
mythology.

White sheets, faintly audible.
His lips move.

You are sick, but you recover.

This is my diary of the last days.

HIGH SPIRITS

The little oak knoll.
A mahogany bureau that cost her fifty dollars.
A featherbed, a deep snow

where oxen strain the engines
whelped of tracks

and life goes—where it goes.

This fear decidedly nubile
forming wherever it lends frame.

The afternoon was pleasant they spoke
of returning home,

of curtains draped
on the four-square knoll

and fireflies hung in windows.

Lanterns all night this fear in me.
Scent of pine and other phantoms.

SCAFFOLDING

A drop born to barefoot
four, coats folding

the knees of spectators.

More soldiers below, the war
over.

And when the world invents photography, the world
is utterly—

thought the past a point
you could return to,

must have gotten that idea from photographs.

Millions, their black-and-white eyes.

Wooden flats still
acrid, scent

of their boots in mud.

What kind of eyes bend over
the print, developing

chemical stain?

MY CHILDHOOD HOME I SEE AGAIN

For each muscling
away, elemental, the sun

descends the flattened harbor,

an expanse I have dreamed
unified.

And still, as memory crowds my brain,
there's pleasure in it—

Our ferry rides the water
strung in lights

when typhoon waves keel sideways—

A vacant wall.
A gilded saloon.

And saddened with the view lodged
behind my right eye

where only a bullet
streams through.

RETURN

Made of all the structures in my life
anxious ego.

Stayed well beyond midnight in the attic
crawl space, daubing

boughs of his roof.

It may rain, you never know.
It may thunder.

Best to be careful.

But only the poor poet weeps, only the moralist
is outraged by the mortal.

"Through the blank wall of timeliness there breaks
and enters a figure to craft the world of forms."

True being, meanwhile, is not in shapes
but in the dreamer.

EMANATIONS-DISSOLUTIONS

A daughter of troubled sleep, this becomes my sense
of purpose.

Where formerly I was a causal
body, now I am borne

in dream's hard-
faceted pupil.

As legend opens the light
of recorded time, these are cabins

he lived through,
places that were his background.

Here he earned his dollar ferrying
triangle elm:

cluster of shoreline
sandstone.

At night the bed opens, a flaming rim
I pass within.

. . .

I know not what propels me. I know not where I move. My uncoordinated soul sees only the leaves of the elm beginning to murmur, willed into water and proceeding to swim. This milk-white rain descends, and I follow the wave of creek water which is the gift wave.

. . .

O ye in the little barge

desirous to listen, have followed

behind my craft

NOTES & ACKNOWLEDGMENTS

Night-Sea samples language from Joseph Campbell's *The Hero With A Thousand Faces*, John T. Morse Jr.'s *Abraham Lincoln*, and *The Inferno of Dante*.

"Half-alligator, half-horse," is from a description of Abraham Lincoln's face.

Lantau Island is off the coast of Hong Kong; Aberdeen is a village on Hong Kong Island.

On the 14th of April, "Ruination Day," Abraham Lincoln was killed by John Wilkes Booth.

Thank you, Juliet Patterson and Laressa Dickey, for reading drafts of these poems.

Thank you, Joni Tevis and David Bernardy, for mimosas on the front stoop and for your shared love of the past.

My gratitude to Ander Monson for his belief in this book.

RACHEL MORITZ is the author of *The Winchester Monologues* (New Michigan Press, 2005). Her poetry has appeared in many journals including *Colorado Review, Denver Quarterly, HOW2, Hayden's Ferry Review, Indiana Review*, and *26*. She lives in Minneapolis, where she publishes chaplets and broadsides for WinteRed Press. She also edits poetry for *Konundrum Engine Literary Review*.

❋

NEW MICHIGAN PRESS, based in Tucson, Arizona, prints poetry and prose chapbooks, especially work that transcends traditional genre. Together with DIAGRAM, NMP sponsors a yearly chapbook competition.

DIAGRAM, a journal of text, art, and schematic, is published bimonthly at <http://thediagram.com>. Periodic print anthologies are available from the New Michigan Press.

❋

COLOPHON

Text is set in a digital version of Jenson, designed by Robert Slimbach in 1996, and based on the work of punchcutter, printer, and publisher Nicolas Jenson.

www.ingramcontent.com/pod-product-compliance
Lightning Source LLC
Chambersburg PA
CBHW031429040426
42444CB00006B/751